Fascist Tendencies in the Congress Party

Fascist Tendencies in the Congress Party

A. Surya Prakash

PRABHAT PRAKASHAN
ISO 9001: 2015 Publishers

Published by
PRABHAT PRAKASHAN
4/19 Asaf Ali Road,
New Delhi-110 002 (INDIA)
e-mail: prabhatbooks@gmail.com

ISBN 978-93-5322-015-0
FASCIST TENDENCIES IN THE CONGRESS PARTY
by A. Surya Prakash

Edition
First, December 2018

Price
₹ 95.00 (Rupees Ninety Five only)

Printed at
R-Tech Offset Printers, Delhi

Content

Introduction

The Congress Party has often spoken against fascism and fascist tendencies. Members of this party are also given to accusing other parties and political leaders of displaying fascist tendencies, but the reality is entirely different.

As the three chapters in this book will show that no party has displayed fascist tendencies more than the Congress Party.

The first chapter is about the shocking instance of the Congress Party's Home Minister praising Hitler and the party's Parliamentary wing working overtime to remove his remarks from the records of parliament. But, the party does not entirely succeed because of my decision to report the incident in the newspaper I worked for. The Home Minister was then forced to tender an apology the next day and democratic India got to know the respect that senior leaders of the Congress Party have for dictators.

Strangely, the party chose this very person for the office of President of India a few months after this incident! Do we need any more evidence of the party's disrespect for democratic traditions?

In the second chapter, 'The Congress and the

Hijackers,' the Congress Party displays its utter disrespect democracy and democratic values when it honours two hijackers and repeatedly gives them party tickets.

The third chapter deals with the dreaded Emergency and the ruthless dictatorship that Indira Gandhi imposed on the country for 21 months, between 1975 and 1977. This chapter is split into different parts to highlight the impact of fascist policies on the judiciary, the Parliament, the media and the executive.

India's founding fathers had warned citizens of such exigencies, like the Emergency, if they were not alert. Dr. Sarvepalli Radhakrishnan, a member of the Constituent Assembly, said, "Our opportunities are great but let me warn you that when power outstrips ability, we will fall on evil days...a free India will be judged by the way in which it will serve the interests of the common man...unless we destroy corruption in high places, root out every trace of nepotism, love of power...we will not be able to raise the standards of efficiency in administration..."[1]

This warning holds good for all time. Fortunately, the people used the first opportunity that came their way in 1977 to restore democracy. The threat from dynasticism, nepotism and corruption to India's much-cherished democracy is not over yet. We need to be ever on our guard. The purpose of this chapter is to keep the flame of eternal vigil alive.

Finally, since the issue is fascism, a word about Sonia Gandhi and her democratic credentials, as she held the office of Congress president for the longest tenure.

Sonia Gandhi is the daughter of Stefano Maino, a building contractor who lived in Orbassano, near Turin in northern Italy. The Mainos were an orthodox Catholic family and Mr. Maino was an ardent admirer and supporter of the Italian fascist dictator Benito Mussolini and the Italian Fascist Party. He fought alongside Hitler's Wehrmacht on the Russian front in World War II. In 1977, after Indira Gandhi's dictatorial regime was ousted from power, Javed Laiq, an Indian journalist visited Maino at his home. Mr. Maino had bound volumes of Mussolini's teachings in his drawing room and he reminisced about the good old days. He told Laiq that except the neo-fascists, he had no respect for the other liberal, democratic parties in Italy. All these parties he said were 'traitors'! This is the political environment in which Sonia Gandhi grew up. It also establishes the ideological compatibility between Indira Gandhi and her daughter-in-law, Sonia! Also, given this reality, is it not strange that Sonia Gandhi goes on talking about fascist forces in India!

Notes:

1. *Constituent Assembly of India Debates (Proceedings)*, Volume V, August 14, 1947, p. 8

❑

I

The Congress Party and Hitler

Ever since Indira Gandhi assumed the role of a dictator during the Emergency and mutilated India's democratic constitution to such an extent that it was beyond recognition, there was always a lurking suspicion that while members of the Congress Party paid lip service to democracy, they were actually inclined towards fascism. Thus, whenever the opportunity arose or when caught off guard, members of this party would bare their fangs and show their true colours.

The most shocking display of such fascination and respect for fascism by a very senior member of the Indira Gandhi cabinet happened in the Lok Sabha on March 24, 1982.

The house was debating the Demands for Grants of the Ministry of Home Affairs that day and the Home Minister, Giani Zail Singh was called by the Deputy Speaker, who was chairing the session, to respond to the issues raised by the members. A few minutes into his speech, Mr. Zail Singh decided to talk about things he and his party truly believed in. To the utter dismay of those in the Opposition benches and the press gallery, Mr. Singh began singing praises of Adolf Hitler and Benito Mussolini. He praised their tenacity of purpose and the discipline they introduced in their countries. He described Hitler as a *Mahaan Vyakti* (a great man) and a *Mahaan Deshbhakt* (a great patriot) and as the builder of modern Germany.

Since the minister was speaking late evening after the house had been through an arduous debate on the working of the Ministry of Home Affairs, many members were in a somnambulant mood and most MPs were anxiously looking at the clock and hoping that the minister's ritualistic reply would be over and done with in a short while. Since a whip had been issued to ensure the presence of all their MPs, the Congress benches were full while the Opposition benches were sparsely filled. None in the treasury or Opposition benches expected any fireworks. After a hard day's work, they just wanted the formality of the minister's speech and the vote on the Demands for Grants of that ministry to be gone through, so that they could head back to their official quarters in Lutyens' Delhi.

In other words, the passage of the Demands for Grants of various ministries was an annual parliamentary rite that had to be performed as ordained by the rule book and the sooner it was over, the better.

But, they were all pulled out of their stupor when Chandrajit Yadav, a socialist and member of one of the breakaway factions of the Janata Party, drew the attention of the Deputy Speaker, Mr. Lakshmanan to Mr. Zail Singh's remarks and asked him to stop the minister in his tracks. Some members of the Congress too woke up to the situation and demanded that the minister's remarks praising Hitler should be expunged. Until Mr. Yadav blew the whistle, the Deputy Speaker too was oblivious to the 'perceptive' observations of the Home Minister. He immediately realised that if the remarks remained on the records of the house, it would do permanent damage to the image of the Congress Party. Although the observations of the Home Minister were not defamatory (they were just laudatory of Hitler) or against any rule of the house, Mr. Lakshmanan took a snap decision to expunge the remarks. Several members of the Opposition protested against the Deputy Speaker's decision but the latter refused to yield to their entreaties. Within minutes of the expunction decision, the Deputy Speaker sent the press officer of the Lok Sabha to the press gallery to inform mediapersons of the expunction and to warn them not to publish a word of what the minister had said about Hitler.

I was the parliamentary correspondent of the *Indian Express* and was reporting the proceedings of the Lok Sabha that day. The press officer conveyed the Deputy Speaker's directions generally to all those present in the press gallery and then walked up to me and said, "Mr. *Indian Express*, I hope you have heard the Deputy Speaker's order!" I said, "Of course, I have heard it!"

Ironically, Mr. Zail Singh made these laudatory references to Hitler while trying to counter the allegation of an Opposition MP, Mr. Niren Ghosh of the Communist Party of India (Marxist), that the country was heading towards total dictatorship and asked the Congress Party if it wished to follow in the footsteps of Hitler. Mr. Zail Singh refuted the charge and said, "We are not moving to dictatorship and the government has no intention to introduce a presidential form of government." He claimed that the Congress Party had never discussed changing the constitution and that Indira Gandhi was 'the most democratic' leader. This was indeed a false claim given the dictatorship imposed by Indira Gandhi between 1975-77, consequent to the Emergency and the shocking constitutional amendments which she introduced at that time, which had robbed the democratic constitution of its very soul.

However, although he did the mandatory lip service to democracy, he could not hold back his true feelings towards Adolf Hitler and spoke freely about how he admired the Fuehrer.

After the rumpus in the house, the much-chastened minister abandoned his enchantment with Hitler and resumed his speech on the work of the Ministry of Home Affairs. I returned to my office, called the editor, Mr. Nihal Singh and told him of what had transpired in the Lok Sabha that evening. I told him that although the Deputy Speaker had expunged the remarks, it was incumbent on us, in public interest, to report what had happened and face the consequences. I told him that my report of the proceedings could result in cancellation of my Lok Sabha pass, but more importantly, it could attract Breach of Privilege notices against the editor, publisher and correspondent. Mr. Singh heard me and without the slightest hesitation, said, "Go ahead."

I put out the story that Home Minister Zail Singh had praised Hitler during his speech in the Lok Sabha and that the Deputy Speaker, bowing to pressure from the Congress benches, had expunged the remarks. It was carried prominently in many editions of the *Indian Express* the next morning on the front page. The headline in the Delhi edition said: *Zail Singh Praises Hitler,*

Everything Expunged. [1]

I woke up to many congratulatory messages from many colleagues within the organisation who were aware of the drama the previous evening, but I had become persona non grata for correspondents of other newspapers who covered the Lok Sabha, for having violated the Deputy Speaker's directions and thereby putting them in a situation whereby they had to explain to their editors as to why they had not reported the incident. As a result, I got a cold reception when I took my seat in the press gallery the next morning. Some correspondents seated nearby warned me that several Congress MPs had given Breach of Privilege notices against the newspaper and that my goose was cooked!

As soon as Question Hour ended, there was much tension in the house as many MPs drew the attention of the Speaker, Mr. Balram Jakhar to their Breach of Privilege notices against the *Indian Express*, while leading members of the Opposition questioned the Deputy Speaker's decision to expunge Mr. Zail Singh's remarks when they did not violate any parliamentary rule. Some Opposition MPs even accused the Home Minister of having violated the oath he had taken under the constitution.

Mr. Madhu Dandavate pointed out that under Article 99 of the Constitution of India, every member of the House, including the Home Minister, had taken an oath of allegiance to the Constitution of India, which believes in the democratic system. Therefore, when Mr. Zail Singh "says anything counter to the spirit of the constitution, by praising or saying something which is commendatory to Hitler's fascist system, it runs counter to the spirit of the (Indian) constitution."[2]

He also took exception to the expunction of the Home Minister's remarks the previous evening and said under the rules of the house, any words which are defamatory, unparliamentary and indecent can be expunged by the presiding officer. The Speaker's powers in this regard are not unlimited. They are governed by the rules.[3]

As the verbal clash between the ruling party and the Opposition intensified, the Speaker informed the house that the Home Minister would make a statement. The Law Minister, Mr. Shiv Shanker, who was seated next to Mr. Zail Singh pulled out a note from his file and gave it to the latter to read. Far from challenging the *Indian Express* for reporting his remarks, the Home Minister tendered an abject apology for praising Hitler the previous day. He said he regretted his remarks about Hitler and was withdrawing those remarks. He said: "Sir, I seek to clarify about what happened yesterday during the course of my reply to the debate on the Demands for Grants of Home Ministry. My extempore observation about Hitler then was only provoked by the heat and the impulse of the debate." He then went on to assert that his party had always fought against fascism, imperialism, racism, etc. and said, "the remarks and observations made by me were unintentional...and off the cuff and did not mean to convey my real feelings, thoughts and sentiments. I regret for all that transpired and withdraw my expressions about Hitler. This is to explain myself and set the record straight."[4]

The Opposition benches responded with loud protests and the Speaker sought to pacify them by saying that the Home Minister was withdrawing his remarks. "He has expressed regret as well as withdrawal," the Speaker said. This led to a fresh bout of exchanges between him and prominent MPs in the Opposition benches. Mr. Atal Behari Vajpayee, the leader of the Bharatiya Janata Party (BJP) cryptically asked the Speaker: "Expunge *kardiya to, withdraw kaise kar sakthe ho* (if the remarks have been expunged, how can he withdraw them now?). He further told the Speaker "This is not the way to run the house. Whatever has been expunged, you bring it back to the proceedings."[5]

Mr. Madhu Dandavate, Mr. Harikesh Bahadur and several others in the Opposition benches protested against the expunction order of the Deputy Speaker and demanded that the Speaker rescind that order and restore the Home Minister's remarks on Hitler in the house's proceedings. Mr. Harikesh Bahadur vociferously told the Speaker, "What has been expunged cannot be withdrawn...when it is not on record, what is he withdrawing." He said the Deputy Speaker cannot exercise his powers arbitrarily.[6]

The minister's statement led to a fresh uproar in the House. Mr. Atal Behari Vajpayee of the Bharatiya Janata Party and Mr. Madhu Dandavate of the Janata Party told the Speaker that they were unable to understand as to what the apology was all about, since his remarks the previous evening had been expunged. They demanded that the expunged portions be restored so that the apology would make sense. Mr. Vajpayee said this was not the first time the Deputy Speaker had erred, "Only recently, he had expunged his own remarks."[7]

Thereafter, the Speaker announced that he had received many breach of privilege notices against the *Indian Express*. He read out a brief order citing rules of the house which prohibit publication of expunged remarks and said the media should always be conscious of it and adhere to it. He chided the *Indian Express* for having violated the orders of the Deputy Speaker. However, he said, in view of the statement (apology) made by the Home Minister, he was dismissing all the notices given by the members against the newspaper!

Thus ended a rather tense hour for me in the Lok Sabha press gallery, but I was happy that I had managed to put the Home Minister's real feelings towards Hitler in the public domain. The next day, newspapers across the country reported all that had transpired on March 25 including the Home Minister's apology and alluded to the minister's remarks on Hitler the previous day.

Neither Indira Gandhi nor anyone else took umbrage at the Home Minister's fascination for Hitler and Mussolini. Instead, just two months after this incident, Indira Gandhi chose Zail Singh as the candidate for the office of President of India. When his candidature was announced, Mr. Singh declared his unswerving loyalty to Indira Gandhi and said he was willing to sweep the floor, if she ordered him to. Mr. Singh won the election effortlessly and took oath as the President of India on July 25, 1982.

Notes:

1. See 'Zail Singh Praises Hitler, Everything Expunged', Indian Express, Delhi Edition, March 25, 1982
2. Col. 284, Lok Sabha Debates, March 25, 1982
3. Col. 283, ibid
4. Col. 289, ibid
5. Col. 289-290, ibid
6. Col. 290, ibid
7. Ibid

❑

II

The Congress and the Hijackers

On December 20, 1978, Bhola Pandey of Azamgarh and his friend Devendar Pandey of Ballia hijacked Indian Airlines flight IC 410 from Lucknow to Delhi soon after it took off from Lucknow. There were 132 passengers on board. The hijackers, who appeared to be armed, made several demands and forced the aircraft to land at Varanasi. They said they were members of the Youth Congress. They wanted Indira Gandhi to be released from jail; all criminal cases against her and Sanjay Gandhi to be withdrawn; and the Janata Party government at the Centre to tender its resignation. They demanded that the authorities should convey their regards to Sanjay Gandhi and summon the Chief Minister of the state for talks. The Chief Minister of Uttar Pradesh, the Inspector General of Police and the Chief Secretary took a special flight to Varanasi and arrived at that airport soon after 1 a.m. the following morning, to negotiate the release of the passengers. The hijackers also demanded that arrangements be made for them to address a press conference at the airport lounge and that the Prime Minister and All India Radio should be informed of the hijacking.

Following protracted negotiations with the Chief Minister and senior state officials, the two hijackers released the passengers and surrendered.

Both the hijackers have been rewarded repeatedly by the Congress Party with party tickets to contest Uttar Pradesh assembly and Lok Sabha elections.

When the Lok Sabha met on December 21, the hijack was on top of everyone's mind. Several members sought an immediate discussion. Prime Minister Morarji Desai told the Speaker he had no objection to a debate "because it is the most serious thing that has happened." Mr. K.P. Unnikrishnan said the hijacking incident was indicative of a far deeper malaise that was creeping into the political firmament, namely "the climate of violence that is being deliberately created..."[1] It was then agreed that the house would have a full-fledged discussion after the minister-in-charge made a statement on the hijacking of the aircraft and its aftermath.

The Minister of Tourism and Civil Aviation Mr. Purushottam Kaushik explained the sequence of events beginning with the hijack of the aircraft soon after it took off from Lucknow the previous day. That week was marked by large-scale violence in many states triggered by members of the Congress Party in protest against the arrest of Mrs. Indira Gandhi in a breach of privilege case and her disqualification from Parliament on December 19. She was sentenced to imprisonment till the prorogation of the house and also expelled from the Lok Sabha. The Pandeys hijacked the plane on December 20 to protest against Parliament's decision to punish Mrs. Gandhi. On December 21, Congress mobs went to the extent of hurling bombs into the Calcutta residence of Mr. Samar Guha, the chairman of the Committee of Privileges of the Lok Sabha, which had indicted Mrs. Gandhi. Congress goons also went on rampage in Bangalore and Hyderabad and targeted public property. Several persons were killed in these incidents. These violent incidents became the subject matter of an intense debate on December 23, 1978 in the Lok Sabha.

Mr. Kaushik told the house that the flight IC 410 took off from Lucknow at 17.45 hrs on December 20. Five minutes later, the flight control centre got a message that some passengers were trying to force their entry into the cockpit. At 18.18 hrs, Lucknow reported that the flight was being hijacked to Patna. Subsequently, Varanasi reported that the flight was landing at that airport and not at Patna. The flight landed at Varanasi at 19.01 hrs. The local police cordoned off the aircraft and the services of a psychiatrist were requisitioned from the Defence authorities. There were 132 passengers on board. Soon after the hijacking was reported, the Central Anti-Hijacking Committee assembled in the control room in Delhi to issue necessary directions on how the hijackers should be dealt with.

While all this was on, one passenger – Mr. Modi – managed to escape from the aircraft with the help of an air hostess and told those in the Varanasi Airport Control Tower that two persons – one wearing a white pyjama and *kurta* and another wearing a white *dhoti* and *kurta* – had boarded the aircraft and they carried printed pamphlets in Hindi and English containing demands for release of the 'national leader' and seeking wide publicity for their actions. The hijackers identified themselves as

Bhola Nath Pandey of Azamgarh and Davender Pandey of Ballia and said they were from the Youth Congress. They wanted the Chief Minister of Uttar Pradesh to reach the Varanasi Airport; arrangements must be made for them (the hijackers) to hold a press conference in the airport lounge; and All India Radio must be informed of the hijacking. The Air Traffic Control at Varanasi kept up the conversation with the hijackers via the pilot, Captain Batliwala. Since the hijackers demanded the presence of the Chief Minister of Uttar Pradesh, the Chief Minister left Lucknow by a state aircraft for Varanasi around midnight and landed in Varanasi at 1.02 hrs. He was accompanied by the Chief Secretary, the Inspector-General of Police and a relative of one of the hijackers. The hijackers declined the request of the authorities to allow women and children to de-board or to allow serving of food and tea to the passengers. The hijackers, in turn, wanted the Chief Minister to enter the aircraft alone, which was not accepted. Finally, arrangements were made for them to talk to the Chief Minister. They demanded that Indira Gandhi should be released forthwith and all criminal cases against her must be withdrawn; the Janata Party government must tender its resignation; and lastly, that the aircraft should proceed back to Lucknow and they must be allowed to meet the press. The Chief Minister agreed to take them to Lucknow in the state aircraft if all the passengers were released. The hijackers initially rejected the Chief Minister's offer and demanded that the aircraft be refuelled. The Central Committee told the negotiators in Varanasi not to refuel the aircraft and to continue negotiations.

Sometime later, the hijackers released some

passengers and demanded that the U.P. state aircraft be brought alongside the Indian Airlines plane. Eventually, they released all the passengers, surrendered their 'weapons' and boarded the state aircraft. The hijackers landed at Lucknow at 8.03 hrs on December 21. On their arrival at Lucknow, the two hijackers were hoping for a big media event but just two reporters and three cameramen turned up to hear their story and they "looked disappointed at the poor press response."[2] The police then took them into custody.

The House took up a full-fledged discussion on the hijacking and the climate of violence in various parts of the country, on December 23.

Initiating the discussion, K.P. Unnikrishnan said the hijacking was a political act by persons associated with the Congress (I) Party (as the Congress led by Indira Gandhi was called at that time) and not an isolated act committed by some mindless young men. He said he condemned the conduct of these hijackers and told MPs belonging to the Congress (I) also to condemn it "because we have to protect certain democratic norms, certain values and way of life, which is at stake today." He said these two hijackers were closely working with a confidant of Indira Gandhi to oust former H.N. Bahuguna, former Chief Minister of Uttar Pradesh and were also active in a *shramdan* camp in Amethi. He said there was a clear pattern of political conduct in what the hijackers had done and the violence that had erupted all over the country was "basically taking the shape of a movement against legitimate functioning of Parliament" (punishing a person for breach of privilege). "The moment a decision is taken in a parliamentary democracy...there are certain parameters of dissent and you cannot cross them, if you want parliamentary democracy to survive."[3] He said the hijackers passed through security without being checked.

MPs belonging to other political parties condemned the hijacking and said that such trends smacked of fascist tendencies, which the Congress Party had in any case displayed in abundant measure during the dreaded Emergency, imposed by Indira Gandhi for 21 months from June 1975. Mr. Kanwarlal Gupta wondered whether in view of the hijacking and violence triggered by the Congress Party, democracy would survive in the country. "It is a question of democracy versus fascism, democracy versus dictatorship," he said.[4]

However, leading lights of the Congress Party including Mr. R. Venkataraman, who later became President of India and Mr. Vasant Sathe, sought to rationalise the conduct of their party members and even tried to dismiss the hijacking incident as nothing more than a joke.

Leaders of this party went to extraordinary lengths to defend Bhola Pandey and Davender Pandey during this debate, which was revealing in terms of the respect that the Congress Party had for Parliament and its committees. It showed that despite the humiliating defeat of the party in the March 1977 Lok Sabha election, when it was punished for imposing a dictatorship on India, the Congress (I) Party had learnt no lessons. The debate once again exposed the Congress mindset, its fascist inclinations and revealed a lot about the party's respect for the rule of law.

Among those who stood up to defend the violence

unleashed by the party was Congress veteran R. Venkataraman, who went so far as to talk about the right of every citizen to express dissent. He said there was a sharp opinion in the country that the punishment meted out to Indira Gandhi was harsh and disproportionate and this had caused resentment in the country and "this resentment has given expression to itself in various ways."

"It is a lesson we have learnt from Gandhiji...when in South Africa, he protested against discriminatory laws and courted imprisonment...When Gandhiji broke the salt laws in the country for the purpose of agitating the people's right to freedom, he exercised the right to dissent. Therefore, the people of the country feel that a certain punishment is out of proportion or is unwarranted (expulsion of Indira Gandhi from the Lok Sabha and her arrest) and they have a right to dissent and to take recourse to such things as to bring forth their point of view. ..."[5]

After this near shameful justification of countrywide violence, including the hijacking, Mr. Venkataraman claimed that the Congress Working Committee had passed a resolution condemning violence. However, "if in spite of it (the resolution), certain people take to certain measures, it is not because of the bidding, it is in spite of it." Therefore, he claimed, the party was not to blame. He then went on to claim that "there are always recalcitrant and intransigent elements in every party. There are always extreme elements in every party and extreme elements cannot be shown or brought up as an argument for condemning the party as a whole."[6]

This argument later sounded hollow because the

Congress Party went on to reward "the recalcitrant and intransigent and extreme elements" — the hijackers — with party tickets to contest not just the state assembly election in Uttar Pradesh but the Lok Sabha polls four times in a row! It shows that those who hijacked the aircraft in 1978 are deeply loved and respected by the Nehru-Gandhis and the Congress Party.

Finally, Mr. Venkataraman dismissed the hijacking as nothing more than a joke. He said when they first heard the news about the hijacking, there was great deal of anger in the country. "But, ultimately, when it turned out to be nothing more than a toy pistol and a cricket ball, sir, it has become the joke of the year." On hearing this, the Speaker said, "Fortunately you were not in the plane."[7]

Mr. Vasant Sathe, another senior parliamentarian in the Congress ranks, said at the outset that he was not justifying the conduct of the Pandeys but said he did not know how to describe the incident. Was it hijacking, skyjacking or sky joking?

According to him, it was "a prank by misguided young men" because they had deployed only a cricket ball and a toy pistol. Mr. Janardhan Poojary blamed the ruling Janata Party government for the violence that culminated in the hijacking. He said there was an overwhelming sentiment across the country in favour of Indira Gandhi and people were willing to sacrifice their lives and their property for her sake.

Lok Sabha records show that Mr. K.P. Unnikrishnan informed the house of the political connections and antecedents of the two Pandeys. He said they were closely connected with a confidant of Indira Gandhi and were 'very active' in the campaign to oust Mr. Bahuguna from the chief ministership of Uttar Pradesh.[8]

Mr. Yadvendra Dutt spoke of how members of the Congress Party were saying that "if Indiraji goes to jail, rivers of blood will flow." The Congress had just a singlepoint programme. "release the queen bee or the honey bees will die. Is this not sycophancy of the highest order?"

Mr. Dutt compared the Congress hooligans to the jackbooted storm-troopers who marched on the streets of Munich and Hamburg during Hitler's reign to create the impression that democracy was useless. "That is exactly what they want to show...that Mrs. Gandhi (is) above law and...above everything."[9] He said Indian Airlines flights must have armed guards and hijackers must be shot dead.

Dr. Saradish Roy said when the house was to take up discussion on the report of the Privileges Committee regarding the breach of privilege committed by Indira Gandhi, the Congress Party made it known that if she was punished by the Lok Sabha, "the roads will be flooded with blood." He accused Mrs. Gandhi of trying to reverse a decision of Parliament through street action. He said she rigged the elections in West Bengal in 1972 and ran the state through a brutal 'a semi-fascist regime'. "All those who opposed her...were assassinated."[10]

Mr. Saugata Roy said Mr. Dharam Bir Sinha, a former MP was on the hijacked plane. He told him that the hijackers were dressed in Khadi *kurta* and *pyjama*. They came out of the cockpit and addressed the passengers and told them why they were hijacking the plane. They said they wanted to focus the attention of the world on

Mrs. Gandhi's arrest. "There may not have been specific instructions, but these young men had a specific purpose in mind — to demand the release of Mrs. Gandhi." He said he heard from Varanasi that groups of Congress Party supporters went to the Varanasi airport that day and raised slogans like, "*Pandey ji ki jai.*"[11]

Mr. P.G. Mavalankar, a member of the Committee of Privileges which found Indira Gandhi guilty of breach of privilege of the house, said, "There was ample proof of her guilt." He did some plain speaking and said he was shocked to hear of the bomb attack on the house of Mr. Samar Guha, chairman, Committee of Privileges. He said the house must stand as one and condemn this incident and build up public opinion against such behaviour. He said neither Mr. Guha nor other members of the Committee of Privileges would be intimidated by such conduct. He said such protests were highly objectionable "as they lead to disruption, dislocation and sabotage and we cannot tolerate it." He said some public decency and standards of morality had to be maintained in politics. Mr. Mavalankar was also amused at Mr. Venkataraman talking of the right of dissent in a democracy after Indira Gandhi had crushed dissent during the Emergency and jailed MPs who spoke against her in Parliament.[12]

Prime Minister Morarji Desai lambasted Mr. Venkataraman and other Congress MPs who were trying to downplay the hijacking. He said it was fortunate that the incident did not end in a disaster. "If the pilots had lost their nerve, anything could have happened." This was the gravity of the hijacking. He said he was pained to hear Mr. Venkataraman's comment that the incident was a joke. "How was it a joke? Such a thing can never be defended, whether it was a toy pistol or whether a ball was presented as a bomb. How was it possible for the pilot to know that it was a toy pistol? They could not take a risk. If anything had happened, I do not know how many lives would have been lost."[13] He also referred to the large-scale violence unleashed by the Congress Party in the country including the bomb attack on the house of the chairman of the Committec of Privileges in the Lok Sabha; the violence in Karnataka, the attack on the house of another MP, Mr. Shejwalkar in Gwalior the previous night; and attempts to burn the office of the Janata Party in Delhi.

He said the hijacking was not just the work of two irresponsible boys. "There are bound to be people behind it because I know messages which have been sent by them." The Prime Minister was hinting at the involvement of other people, possibly higher-ups in the party's hierarchy.[14]

The Congress hatched a plot to split the Janata Party in Parliament in 1979 and succeeded in doing so by weening away Chaudhary Charan Singh and his followers. The Congress Party tempted him with prime ministership if he broke away with his MPs. It offered him support to form the government. These moves led to the fall of the Morarji Desai government. Mr. Charan Singh was sworn in as Prime Minister by the President, but he never faced the Parliament as Prime Minister because the Congress Party withdrew support before the next session and thus forced elections. Meanwhile, the Charan Singh government, under pressure from the Congress Party, initiated the process to withdraw the case against the hijackers.

The case against the two Pandeys was dropped. Thereafter, the Congress Party honoured both of them by giving them tickets in the 1980 Uttar Pradesh assembly election. They were elected to the state assembly. Davendra Pandey has also held key posts in the Uttar Pradesh Congress Committee. They were again given party tickets in the state assembly election held in 1989. Since then, Bhola Pandey has been a favourite of the Nehru-Gandhis and has got the Congress Party ticket to contest the Lok Sabha elections from Salempur constituency in Uttar Pradesh five times: in 1991, 1999, 2004, 2009 and 2014. On all these occasions, he has been unsuccessful but the party has consistently reposed faith in him. Further, Bhola Pandey has had his brush with the law on several occasions since the hijacking. For example, he was arrested and remanded to judicial custody by a local court in Ballia in March 2009, following a non-bailable warrant in an extortion case dating back to 1982. Though remanded to judicial custody, the magistrate permitted him to file his nomination papers for the Lok Sabha election.

However, his clout with the Nehru-Gandhis is such that he was once again given the ticket for the Salempur Lok Sabha seat in 2014! Who knows? Given their persistence, the Nehru-Gandhis may well succeed in their efforts to bring the man who hijacked a plane in 1978 into their ranks in Parliament!

Notes:

1. Col. 326-327, *Lok Sabha Debates*, December 21, 1978
2. Col. 331-335, *Lok Sabha Debates*, December 21, 1978
3. Cols. 2-7, *Lok Sabha Debates*, December 23, 1978
4. Col. 23, *Lok Sabha Debates*, December 23, 1978

5. Cols. 14-17, *Lok Sabha Debates*, December 23, 1978
6. Ibid
7. Ibid
8. Col. 41, *Lok Sabha Debates*, December 23, 1978
9. Cols. 37-40, *Lok Sabha Debates*, December 23, 1978
10. Cols. 28-29, *Lok Sabha Debates*, December 23, 1978
11. Cols. 45-48, *Lok Sabha Debates*, December 23, 1978
12. Cols. 59-60, *Lok Sabha Debates*, December 23, 1978
13. Cols. 107-112, *Lok Sabha Debates*, December 23, 1978
14. Ibid

❑

III

The Emergency : How the Infrastructure was Laid for Dictatorship[1]

Every year, June 25 marks the anniversary of the dreaded Emergency that was imposed by Indira Gandhi to snuff out democracy and to gain absolute power after she was found guilty of corrupt electoral practices. She got a pliant President to issue a proclamation under Article 352 of the constitution to impose an 'Internal Emergency' and thus turned a vibrant democracy into a dictatorship. The Emergency, which lasted 21 months, constituted the darkest hour of India's democracy.

During the Emergency, the constitution was mutilated, Parliament was reduced to a rubber stamp and the media was gagged. Even the judiciary failed to stand up to the tyrannical regime. As a result, the people of India lost their basic freedoms and came face-to-face with fascism.

India's tallest leaders were arrested soon after the President signed the proclamation. Those arrested included Jayaprakash Narayan, Atal Bihari Vajpayee, Chandra Shekhar, Charan Singh, L.K. Advani, Madhu

Dandavate, Ramakrishna Hegde, Morarji Desai, Biju Patnaik, Nanaji Deshmukh, Sikander Bakht, Balasaheb Deoras, the Sarsanghchalak of the Rashtriya Swayamsevak Sangh (RSS) and a large number of other leaders.

As on February 12, 1977, the government said that of the 6,330 persons belonging to banned organisations and political parties who were detained under the Maintenance of Internal Security Act (MISA), 4,026 were from the RSS (3,254) and the Jana Sangh (772).[2]

Many of those who hold prominent positions today suffered jail terms during the Emergency. They include India's Vice-President, Mr. Venkaiah Naidu; Arun Jaitley, the Union Minister for Finance and Corporate Affairs; Prakash Javadekar, Minister for Human Resource Development; Ravi Shankar Prasad, Minister for Law and Justice and Information Technology; Ram Vilas Paswan, Minister for Consumer Affairs, Food and Public Distribution; and Dattatreya Hosabale, senior RSS leader. Subramanian Swamy, the Rajya Sabha MP, was yet another Emergency hero who dodged the police, slipped out of the country twice and campaigned against Indira Gandhi's dictatorship in Europe and the US. The government foisted many cases against him and subjected him to much harassment.

Among those in the Opposition today, H.D. Deve Gowda, former Prime Minister; Lalu Prasad Yadav, leader of the Rashtriya Janata Dal; and Nitish Kumar, Chief Minister of Bihar, were jailed during the Emergency. Prime Minister Narendra Modi was an RSS Pracharak during the Emergency. He led the underground movement and played a key role in helping the families of those jailed by the Indira Gandhi government. He had the responsibility to organise secret meetings of the resistance, distribute literature and keep track of the needs of senior leaders.

The trigger for the anti-corruption movement launched by Jayaprakash Narayan was the Navnirman movement against corruption, which began in Gujarat. Modi and his colleagues in the RSS worked unobtrusively to keep the movement against corruption and against the Emergency going.

My memories of the Emergency go back to that eerie feeling on the morning of June 26, when V.N. Subba Rao, my chief reporter in *The Indian Express,* Bangalore, called to say that an Emergency had been imposed and many national leaders had been arrested. He summoned me to the office to chase these stories. Soon thereafter, we heard that censorship had been imposed and that all our copies had to be sent to the chief censor. Out to humiliate the media, the government appointed the Inspector General of Police (IGP), Karnataka, as the Chief Censor in the state. The IGP had a battery of police inspectors and sub-inspectors and information department officials working as *'chhota censors'*. The 'censors' would run through these copies, cut out anything that looked like criticism of Indira Gandhi or which showed the government in poor light, and return them to the newspaper. The senior editorial staff had to ensure that the censors' instructions were carried out. Thus, the Inspector General of Police became my editor throughout the Emergency!

My other recollection of the Emergency was my meeting with Lawrence Fernandes, brother of George Fernandes, after he was released by the Corps of

Detectives, Karnataka, in March 1977. He had been brutally tortured in police custody and broke down several times during a late-night interview at his Richmond Town home in Bangalore.

When the interview was published, the people were shocked and the Union Government was furious. It directed the editor to carry the government's version on front page the next day. The Indira Gandhi government was confident of returning to power in the election due in March 1977 and the state's Home Secretary echoed this sentiment when he called to say that the government would 'deal' with me after the election results came in. Luckily, Indira Gandhi's Congress was routed in the elections and people voted to restore democracy in the country.

If we are to protect ourselves from such tyranny hereafter, we need to remember the story of the Emergency. It must be told and retold so that the idea of democracy gets replenished, generation after generation.

It would take many volumes to put together a full account of the horrors of the Emergency and to chronicle all the tales of hardship faced by the people during those 21 months. This chapter just provides a glimpse.

Infrastructure Laid for Dictatorship

The political crisis that led to the imposition of the Emergency began on 12 June 1975, when Justice Jagmohan Lal Sinha of the Allahabad High Court held Prime Minister Indira Gandhi guilty of corrupt practice in the Lok Sabha election of 1971. The judge declared her election to Parliament as void and barred her from contesting elections for six years.

Indira Gandhi's lawyers filed an appeal in the Supreme Court. Justice V.R. Krishna Iyer passed orders on this appeal on June 24, but the interregnum was used by the Congress Party to stage a series of rent-a-crowd rallies in support of Indira Gandhi outside her residence. The biggest rally was held on June 20 and for this the Delhi administration and the Delhi Police commandeered 1,700 buses of the Delhi Transport Corporation (DTC) and private transport companies, and the Railways ran special trains from far and near. Since all buses were forcibly requisitioned for the rally, citizens of Delhi had to do without public transport that day.

Indira Gandhi had hoped that the Supreme Court would provide her relief but that was not to be. Justice Iyer granted a 'conditional stay' of Justice Sinha's decision. He barred Indira Gandhi from participating in debates or voting in Parliament and referred the matter to a larger bench of the court.

Meanwhile, the Opposition parties got together to press for Indira Gandhi's resignation in the light of the Allahabad High Court judgement. Justice Iyer's order, prohibiting the Prime Minister from voting in Parliament or participating in debates, had made her position even more untenable, they said, and demanded that she quit office forthwith.

Instead of bowing to the court's verdict, Indira Gandhi decided to cling to office at any cost. As her sycophants vied with each other to produce hired crowds before her house, Indira Gandhi summoned Siddhartha Shankar Ray and told him the country required 'a shock treatment'. Ray said she could give India the shock treatment by imposing an 'Internal Emergency' under

Article 352 of the constitution. Thereafter, Indira Gandhi, accompanied by Ray, went to the President and asked him to impose an Internal Emergency under Article 352. She said there was no time to call a meeting of the Union cabinet to discuss the proposal. On her return from Rashtrapati Bhavan (the presidential residence), she sent a letter to the President accompanied by a proclamation. President Fakhruddin Ali Ahmed signed on the dotted line, violating all procedure.

Once the deed was done, the government cut off electricity to New Delhi's Fleet Street – Bahadur Shah Zafar Marg, to prevent publication of newspapers next morning. A chief censor was appointed to keep a close watch on newspapers and journalists.

After the infrastructure for dictatorship had been laid, other things followed. On June 27 1975, the President issued an order suspending citizens' right to move the courts for enforcement of fundamental rights. Most of those arrested were locked up under the dreaded MISA with officials fabricating charges.

Meanwhile, sycophancy reached its zenith. Deo Kant Barooah, president of the Congress Party, declared 'Indira is India, India is Indira'.

One of the most ugly features of the Emergency was forcible sterilisation of the population and cleaning up of cities on Sanjay Gandhi's instructions. In order to achieve quick results, Sanjay Gandhi assigned sterilisation targets to all Chief Ministers, who in turn passed on targets to all government servants, including teachers and policemen. The police went about target achievement in the only way they knew. They surrounded villages, nabbed all males a la municipal squads which trap street dogs and carted them off to the nearest primary health centres to be vasectomised. When villagers resisted, the police opened fire, killing and injuring many protestors. Katherine Frank, Indira Gandhi's biographer, has mentioned the horror of forcible sterilisation and the scars left on the psyche of the common man. 'Some people were simply coerced – rather than motivated or bribed – to be sterilised. In Delhi, Calcutta, Bombay and other Indian cities, tens of thousands of homeless people lived on the streets. During the Emergency, thousands were arrested for 'vagrancy' and taken off to sterilisation camps where they had no choice but to undergo vasectomies.'[3]

Similar atrocities were perpetrated in the name of cleaning up Delhi. Backed by a strong police force, municipal officials in Delhi swooped on residents of Turkman Gate and other areas and bulldozed hundreds of homes.

Dozens of citizens were killed or injured in the riots that broke out in the area. The conduct of the bureaucracy was pathetic. Bureaucrats close to Sanjay Gandhi threatened Indian Administrative Service (IAS) officers with arrest under MISA, and barring some honourable exceptions, most officers succumbed to the pressure. They meekly complied with all illegal orders and caused endless misery to common people.

Parliament's Assault on the Constitution

If the conduct of the bureaucracy was pathetic, so was that of Parliament. Fearing coercive action by Indira Gandhi and her son, Congress MPs vied with one another to pass some of the most shameful amendments to the constitution, drafted exclusively to help Indira

Gandhi wriggle out of the electoral malpractices case. These amendments were pushed through both houses of Parliament because the government had jailed a number of Opposition MPs. Further, the Congress Party had the support of the Communist Party of India (CPI). This party provided critical support to Indira Gandhi throughout this dictatorial phase.

The first of these amendments – the thirty-eighth amendment – barred judicial review of the Emergency proclamation.

The thirty-ninth amendment was meant solely to pre-empt the Supreme Court of India, which was hearing Indira Gandhi's election case. This extraordinary amendment prohibited the Supreme Court from hearing election petitions against the Prime Minister, Speaker of the Lok Sabha, the President and the Vice President. It said Parliament would establish a body to hear such petitions. Further, it placed all laws pertaining to elections in the Ninth Schedule of the constitution (to bar judicial review) and declared that with the passage of this amendment, all election petitions before courts would abate. This was followed up with the Election Laws Amendment Act passed on August 5, 1975 specifically to nullify the points upheld by Justice Jagmohan Lal Sinha against Indira Gandhi.

But this was just for starters. More was to follow. In the days and months that followed, Parliament was thus consumed in just one activity – making laws to save Indira Gandhi. If this meant a blow against the constitution, so be it. After the thirty-ninth amendment came the fortieth which placed an anti-media law in the Ninth Schedule to bar judicial review. Then came the

Constitution Forty-first Amendment Bill. Introduced in the Rajya Sabha on August 9, 1975, two days before the Supreme Court was to hear India Gandhi's election petition, it amended Article 361 to say:

No criminal proceedings 'whatsoever' could lie in court against a person who is or who had been the President, Prime Minister, or Governor for acts 'done by him, whether before he entered upon his office or during his term of office'. Also, no civil proceedings can lie against persons holding these offices 'in respect of any act done before or after he entered office'.

This extraordinary amendment was passed by the Rajya Sabha on the very day of introduction.

Can any democratic constitution have a provision like this, which places some citizens above or beyond the law?

Among the amendments made to the constitution during the Emergency, the forty-second amendment was the most comprehensive and its primary aim was to clip the wings of the judiciary. It was introduced in the Lok Sabha on September 1, 1976 and after passage through the two houses of Parliament received the President's assent on December 18, 1976. This amendment declared that henceforth any amendment to the constitution cannot be questioned 'in any court on any ground'. It declared that the amendments to the chapter on Fundamental Rights was beyond judicial review and that Parliament's power to amend the constitution is unlimited 'by way of addition, variation or repeal'. This meant that Parliament henceforth had the unfettered power to preserve or destroy the constitution.

Some of the other provisions were: Barring high

courts from ruling on the constitutionality of central laws; barring high courts from issuing stay orders relating to 'any work or project of public utility'; insertion of Article 31D prohibiting 'anti-national activity' and stating that creating 'internal disturbance' and 'disrupting harmony' is anti-national; declaring that no law made in this regard is unconstitutional merely because it is inconsistent with fundamental rights in Articles 14, 19 and 31. Further, in order to avoid any debarment of MPs for electoral malpractices (as in the case of Indira Gandhi), the forty-second amendment said courts cannot disqualify MPs found guilty of corrupt election practices. Henceforth, the President would decide on disqualification after 'consulting' the Election Commission. The amendment also weakened the federal structure when it empowered central forces to operate under Central control when sent to a state to preserve law and order.

As if all this was not enough, the forty-second amendment abolished the need for quorum in Parliament and state legislatures. Until this amendment, the constitution stipulated that the quorum to constitute Parliament and state legislative bodies was 10 per cent of the strength of each house. Once this was done away with, it became technically possible for a single MP to make law for the entire country!

Finally, the most shocking and reprehensible provision in the forty-second amendment was the power it vested in the President for two years to amend these provisions in the constitution, through an executive order! It said if there were any difficulties in giving effect to the constitution as amended, the president may, by order, for up to two years, 'adapt or modify the provision to remove the difficulty'. Through this provision, Parliament had passed on its exclusive power to amend the constitution to the executive.

These were not laws made in Adolf Hitler's Germany or Benito Mussolini's Italy. They were part of a torrent of laws written up in great haste in the first flush of the Emergency to tighten the grip of Indira Gandhi's dictatorship and to wipe out all forms of dissent. Many of these laws and constitutional amendments, which would make the founding fathers of our republic sit up in their graves, were drafted by a bunch of unscrupulous bureaucrats, who were completely devoid of character and commitment to democracy.

Summing up the situation and the plight of Parliament, S.S. Gill, a senior civil servant, said:

"Having imposed Emergency, Indira's first concern was to make herself legally invulnerable. Soon after the event, she suspended constitutional rights regarding equality before law (Art. 14), right of life and liberty (Art. 21), and protection against arbitrary arrest and detention (Art. 22) through a presidential ordinance. A couple of days later, Maintenance of Internal Security Act (MISA) was amended to provide for the detention of a person upto two years without disclosing the grounds for doing so. Further, parliamentary proceedings were censored and rules of procedure suspended. Question Hour and motions by private members were discontinued. When the Parliament met on July 21 for the monsoon session, Opposition MPs were already in jail and two days later most others also walked out. Thus, the PM was left with an emasculated, rump Parliament which approved all the new legislative measures without demur."[4]

How the Judiciary Buckled under Pressure

Our judges often say 'be you ever so high, the law is above you'. This dictum is a fundamental prerequisite in a democracy, but did our judges adhere to it when dealing with the Indira Gandhi government, which was mutilating the constitution? Like the bureaucracy and Parliament, our courts too let us down.

The Supreme Court heard Indira Gandhi's petition from August 11, 1975 and pronounced its judgement a few months later on November 7. The court validated the retrospective character of the thirty-ninth amendment and, consequently, Indira Gandhi's election.

Then came the habeas corpus case. Many detenus including Madhu Dandavate and L.K. Advani approached the high courts, challenging the presidential proclamation and asserting their fundamental rights.

An important case in this genre of cases was *ADM (Additional District Magistrate) Jabalpur v. Shiv Kant Shukla.* The Madhya Pradesh High Court ruled on September 1, 1975 that its right to examine cases of habeas corpus cannot be abridged. The Union Government appealed against this order. The Supreme Court admitted the appeal and decided to take up all such cases which were pending in the high courts. This is known as the habeas corpus case. It was heard by a five judge bench comprising Chief Justice A.N. Ray and Justices H.R. Khanna, M.H. Beg, Y.V. Chandrachud and P.N. Bhagwati. The government argued that a judicial review of these detentions was out of question.

The case was decided on April 28, 1976. Four judges – A.N. Ray, M.H. Beg, Y.V. Chandrachud and P.N. Bhagwati – held that no citizen had the right to move a writ of habeas corpus in the light of the presidential order of June 27, 1975 or to challenge a detention as illegal. Among these judges, Justice Beg went so far as to praise the 'maternal' attitude of the government. He said, "We understand that the care and concern bestowed by the state authorities upon the welfare of detenus who are well-fed and well-treated, is almost maternal. Even parents have to take appropriate preventive action against those children who may threaten to burn down the house they live in."[5]

Justice H.R. Khanna was the only judge who dissented. He found no merit in the government's case.

When Jayaprakash Narayan heard this judgement, he said it had put out the last flickering candle of individual freedom, "Mrs. Gandhi's dictatorship both in its personalised and institutionalised forms is now complete." The number of persons detained during the Emergency under MISA and the Defence of India Act reached a staggering 1,11,000.

The death of democracy in India on June 25, 1975 was best encapsulated in this clever 'obituary notice' put out by a democrat in a Bombay newspaper soon after the presidential proclamation was made public. It said: 'O'cracy D.E.M., beloved husband of T. Ruth, loving father of L.I. Bertie, brother of Faith, Hope, Justice, expired on 26th June.'

However, luckily, the people of India managed to resurrect 'O'cracy D.E.M' in March 1977. Since the media was gagged, Indira Gandhi and Sanjay Gandhi had no authentic sources of information about the prevailing public mood. Going by the daily feed of good news from sycophants, Indira Gandhi ordered elections in March 1977, hoping to return to Parliament and perpetuate her dictatorship. This was however not to be.

The Congress was trounced in this Lok Sabha poll.

Assault on the Media

The first thing the Emergency regime did was to mount an assault on the media. It appointed a chief censor and declared that nothing was to be published without the clearance of the censor's office. The government also classified newspapers as 'friendly', 'neutral' and 'hostile' and began harassing media houses and journalists in the last category.

A large number of journalists were arrested during the Emergency. Many others were subjected to harassment like withdrawal of accreditation. Journalists given to independent thinking were subjected to surveillance by the Intelligence Bureau (IB). Apart from the restrictions placed on the enforcement of fundamental rights, including the right to expression and free speech through the forty-second amendment to the constitution, the Indira Gandhi government took several other legislative measures to browbeat the media. These included the repeal of the Parliamentary Proceedings (Protection of Publication) Act, 1977, the Press Council Act, 1978, and the passage of the Prevention of Publication of Objectionable Matter Act, 1976.

Several editors including B.G. Verghese, chief editor, *Hindustan Times,* V.K. Narasimhan, editor-in-chief, *The Indian Express* and Nikhil Chakravarty, editor, *Mainstream*, lodged complaints of harassment by censor officers. Independent journalists and their family members were harassed, arrested under the Defence of India Rules (DIR) or MISA. Their accreditations were withdrawn and managements were forced to terminate their services. Newspapers which refused to do so were denied government advertisements. In all 253 journalists were arrested during the Emergency: 110 under MISA, 60 under DIR. They included Kuldip Nayyar, K.R. Malkani, Virender Kapur and K.R. Sundararajan.

Most of the time, the government went to ridiculous lengths to protect itself. For example, it banned newspapers from carrying quotations from Tagore, Mahatma Gandhi and Jawaharlal Nehru. This order was issued to prevent newspapers or columnists from referring to speeches or writings of national leaders on freedom, democracy and fundamental rights.

The government also came down heavily on cinema and banned movies, such as *Kissa Kursi Ka, Aandhi* and *Andolan* and prohibited the screening of *All the President's Men,* which showcased the investigative work of journalists against US President Nixon.

The horrors of the Emergency were thereafter documented by the Shah Commission of Inquiry appointed by the Janata Party government.

Some of the biggest villains of the Emergency were part of Sanjay Gandhi's cabal. They included Defence Minister Bansi Lal, Navin Chawla, an IAS officer and police officers P.S. Bhinder and K.S. Bajwa.

Navin Chawla, who was Secretary to Krishan Chand, Lt. Governor of Delhi, became a law unto himself because of his proximity to the Indira Gandhi household. His contribution to the promotion of Indira Gandhi's dictatorship has been highlighted by the Shah Commission, which probed the atrocities of the Emergency.

Shades of Auschwitz

The most damning piece of evidence against Chawla came from the Tihar Jail. There was a heavy rush of political detenus in Tihar Jail after the proclamation of the Emergency and the jail staff had to double the number of prisoners in each barrack. While the jail could accommodate 1,273 inmates, the number had swelled to 3,500 to 4,200. S.K. Batra, the Jail Superintendent, said officials of the Intelligence Bureau, the Central Bureau of Investigation and Delhi Police were allowed to freely visit the jail and meet the detenus without any permission from the jail authorities 'and this was done under the orders of Shri Navin Chawla.'

The commission observed that "though Shri Navin Chawla had no position in the jail hierarchy, he was exercising extra statutory control in jail matters and sending instructions on all matters including the treatment of particular detenus." The Jail Superintendent told the commission that Chawla had suggested the construction of some cells with asbestos roofs to 'bake' certain persons. A proposal to this effect was also processed but given up eventually due to certain technical reasons. Further, Chawla had on one occasion suggested that certain troublesome detenus "should be kept with the lunatics".[6]

The commission said, "Shri Krishan Chand (the Lt. Governor) has also said that the PM had handed over the running of Delhi to Shri Sanjay Gandhi and four-five officers who were close to Shri Gandhi used to receive direct orders from him. He has admitted that whenever some 'instructions' were given to him by Shri Navin Chawla, he took them to be emanating from Shri Sanjay Gandhi."[7]

This is an extraordinary confession by the man who was Delhi's Lieutenant Governor during the Emergency. He admitted that he received 'instructions' from his Secretary, Navin Chawla! Do we need any more evidence to clinch the point that Chawla was indeed the de facto Lieutenant Governor?

Even more disturbing was Navin Chawla's involvement in the Gestapo-style political indoctrination of opponents of the Emergency regime. The Shah Commission found records which showed that a special sub-committee had been constituted 'to interrogate certain persons who had tendered apology for their past political activities'. This sub-committee included a psychiatrist! The commission said the purpose of this interrogation, conducted in jail, was to ascertain the genuineness of the political conversion of these persons. 'Smt. Chandra has stated that this special sub-committee was Shri Navin Chawla's idea. Since no rational explanation was given by the concerned witnesses for constituting such a sub-committee, one wonders if this was an attempt at political indoctrination of the opponents of the Emergency regime,' the commission wondered.[8]

This conclusion of the commission strengthens the view that Chawla played a critical role in the unlawful and unconstitutional decisions that were being taken in Delhi in furtherance of a dictatorship. Krishan Chand, the Lieutenant Governor, said he worked under the directions of Om Mehta, Minister of State for Home Affairs, who was in charge of Delhi. However, "sometimes, Shri Navin Chawla and Shri Bhinder would also bring information from the PM's house and action was taken." Significantly, the LG admitted that his secretary had enormous powers when it came to throwing people in jail! The commission noted that Krishan Chand "agreed with Smt. Chandra's statement regarding the powers enjoyed by Shri Navin Chawla and Shri K.S. Bajwa in matters of detention and said that though no detention orders were issued as such by these officers, whatever they said was accepted."

Shah Commission Indicts Navin Chawla

By way of indicting Navin Chawla, the Shah Commission said, 'It is clear on the evidence that Shri P.S. Bhinder, K.S. Bajwa and Navin Chawla exercised enormous powers during the Emergency because they had easy access to the then Prime Minister's house. Having acquired that power, they used it without considering whether the exercise was moral or immoral, legal or illegal. The commission is of the opinion that though the involvement of these officers may vary slightly in degree, their approach to the problems of the period relating to the citizens was authoritarian and callous. Their only anxiety was to preserve and protect their proximity to the seat of power and towards that end, they did everything which they thought would lead to their own advancement. They grossly misused their position and abused their powers in cynical disregard of the welfare of citizens and in the process rendered themselves unfit to hold any public office which demands an attitude of fair play and consideration for others. In their relish for power they completely subverted the normal channels of command and administrative procedures.'[9]

In its concluding remarks on the conduct of Chawla and other officers during the Emergency, the commission had this to say: 'Effective dissent was smothered, followed by a general erosion of democratic values. High-handed and arbitrary actions were carried out with impunity... Tyrants sprouted at all levels overnight – tyrants whose claim to authority was largely based on their proximity to power...'[10]

The Union Government informed Parliament on May 15, 1978 in its 'Memorandum of Action Taken' that it had 'accepted the findings, observations and recommendations of the commission'. If the Union Government has 'accepted' the recommendations of the commission and told Parliament so, how could Navin Chawla, a man who was declared to be 'authoritarian and callous' and had been declared 'unfit to hold any public office which demands an attitude of fair play' become, of all things, an election commissioner!

Monstrous Folly

Long years after he received this strong indictment at the hands of the Shah Commission, the United Progressive Alliance (UPA) government led by the Congress Party, of which Indira Gandhi's daughter-in-law Sonia Gandhi was the party president and the de facto head of government, appointed him as an Election Commissioner. The Election Commission has the responsibility to not only conduct elections but also to protect political pluralism and deepen democracy. Therefore, a deep and abiding commitment to democracy and the core values in our constitution is a fundamental qualification for a person who is vested with the power of superintendence, direction and control of elections in India. Given the findings of the Shah Commission, the elevation of Chawla to the office of Election Commissioner in 2005 was the ultimate insult one could heap on the constitution and the democratic values enshrined in it. As if this was not enough, Mr. Chawla later became the Chief Election Commissioner!

For all those who have lived through that nightmare called Emergency or have read the report of the Shah Commission of Inquiry that documented the horrific consequences of dictatorship, the appointment of Navin Chawla, a man completely at odds with democracy itself, as an Election Commissioner, constituted a monstrous folly.

Given the Shah Commission's damning indictment of Navin Chawla as 'authoritarian and callous', this decision of the Congress Party is yet another example of the party's fascist rather than democratic inclinations.

We need to find out who mooted the proposal to make Chawla an Election Commissioner? How committed was the promoter of this idea to democracy and the core values of our constitution? Was President A.P.J. Abdul Kalam informed of Chawla's antecedents when the file was put before him? India's constitutional well-being should not have been sacrificed for the sake of a partisan, undemocratic careerist. We do not have answers to these questions as yet. But we do have some clues. As stated in the introductory chapter, Sonia Gandhi, the president of the Congress Party at that time, is the daughter of Stephano Maino, an ardent supporter of Benito Mussolini who fought alongside the Nazis and who had contempt for liberal, democratic parties in Italy later in his life.

Do we need to say more?

Notes:

1. This chapter is an abridgement of a couple of chapters in A. Surya Prakash's book, *The Emergency – Indian Democracy's Darkest Hour*, published by Megh Nirghosh Media
2. *Shah Commission of Inquiry, Interim Report* II, April 1978, p. 39
3. Katherine Frank, *Indira – The Life of Indira Nehru Gandhi*, Harper Perennial, Great Britain, 2001, p. 407
4. S.S. Gill, *The Dynasty–A Political Biography of the Premier Ruling Family of Modern India*, Harper Collins, New Delhi, 1996, p. 271
5. http://indiankanoon.org/doc/1735815
6. *Shah Commission of Inquiry, Interim Report* II, April, 1978, p. 39
7. ibid, p. 46
8. ibid, p. 38
9. ibid, p. 46
10. Ibid

❑

IV
Conclusion

The Shah Commission summed up the aberrations that crept in when it said that effective dissent was smothered and tyrants sprang up everywhere, indulging in high-handed and arbitrary conduct. People lived in such mortal fear of Indira Gandhi and her government that even men like R. Venkataraman, who later became India's President, lacked the courage to speak up during the Emergency. Long years after the Emergency ended, he picked up the courage to finally acknowledge that the Emergency should never have been promulgated.

He said, Indira Gandhi was one of the most dynamic Prime Ministers that India had had and that she was 'a unique personality'. However, "The Emergency interregnum tarnished her, giving her the image of a dictator." According to him, "She was misled into a totally unnecessary and unwarranted action by her closest advisers."[1]

I would be doing grave injustice to the history of the Emergency, if I do not acknowledge the immense contribution of Justice H.R. Khanna, one of the great heroes of the second freedom struggle, before I conclude. This judge not only made an immense sacrifice to preserve core constitutional values and to uphold the democratic rights of citizens, but also fought a lone battle to defend the citizen's right to life and personal liberty even as his brother judges bartered away this right in that forgettable majority-decision of the Supreme Court in what is known as the Habeas Corpus Case (ADM, Jabalpur v. Shiv Kant Shukla).

In that case, the Supreme Court was called upon to determine whether citizens could move courts to safeguard their right under Article 21 of the constitution, when the Emergency was in force. While four of his colleagues on the bench said 'no', Justice Khanna dissented and said "... the constitution and the laws of India do not permit life and liberty to be at the mercy of the absolute power of the executive."

While all the articles in Part III of the constitution dealing with fundamental rights are important, Article 21 is rather special. It says: 'No person shall be deprived of his life and personal liberty except according to procedure established by law.' This is a constitutional provision that highlights the distinction between democracy and dictatorship, between rule of law and the law of the jungle. Such is the importance of this fundamental right that a nation that does not have such a provision in its constitution cannot claim to be a democracy. Yet, the first thing that Indira Gandhi did after she imposed the Emergency was to get the President to rubber-stamp an order suspending all fundamental rights, including the right to life and personal liberty.

Once this order was passed, thousands of political workers, journalists and social activists were jailed by the government and some of them moved the High

Courts challenging this order and claiming that Article 21 cannot be suspended. Many political leaders, such as Lal Krishna Advani and Madhu Dandvate were among the petitioners. The Supreme Court directed the transfer of these cases to itself. A five-judge bench comprising the Chief Justice A.N. Ray and Justices H.R. Khanna, M.H. Beg, Y.V. Chandrachud and P.N. Bhagwati heard these petitions. During the hearing, Niren De, the Attorney General, contended that so long as the Emergency was in force, no citizen could knock on the doors of a court to seek enforcement of the right to life and personal liberty.

Any democrat would have been aghast to hear such an argument. But most of the judges heard the Attorney General in silence. Justice Khanna notes in his autobiography *Neither Roses Nor Thorns* that he found some of his colleagues, who used to be very vocal about human rights and civil liberties, 'were sitting tongue tied' and 'their silence seemed rather ominous'. Justice Khanna therefore decided to confront the Attorney General. He asked him whether, in view of his submissions, there would be any remedy "if a police officer, because of personal enmity, killed another man?" Justice Khanna says the Attorney General's answer was unequivocal. Consistent with his argument, he said, "There would be no judicial remedy in such a case so long as the Emergency lasts." He further said, "It may shock your conscience, it shocks mine, but consistent with my submissions, no proceedings can be taken in a court of law on that score."[2]

Although it 'shocked' the conscience of the Attorney General, it did not stir the conscience of the majority on the bench. Chief Justice Ray and Justices Beg,

Chandrachud and Bhagwati upheld the government's contention that it had the right to suspend the right to life and personal liberty. Justice Khanna dissented. The case raises questions which impact the basic values affecting life, liberty and the rule of law, he said, while rejecting the government's contention.

I am sure that Generation Y or the Millennials (those born after the Emergency nightmare ended) would read some of these stories about the Emergency in total disbelief. Having grown up in the age of the 'Argumentative Indian', the Internet, the no-holds-barred social media and cacophonous television debates, they may find it difficult to comprehend that the Congress Party – India's oldest political party and the party that was at the vanguard of the freedom movement – could have foisted dictatorship on the country and inflicted such cruelty and hardship on the citizens. Their ignorance or lack of understanding of what happened in India during 1975-77 is also due to the fact that this very important chapter in the country's post-independence history is hidden from the post-Emergency generation. This needs to be corrected, if we cherish the core values of our constitution and our democratic way of life. Students in high schools across the country must be told about the Emergency and the findings of the Shah Commission.

Gen Y must know that we had heroes like Jayaprakash Narayan and Justice H.R. Khanna and that it is because of them that we still breathe the free air. Only then will our democracy and our free and liberal spirit remain intact.

Finally, a word about the family-centric attitude of the Congress Party and its consequences for our democratic well-being. I would like to draw the attention of fellow citizens to events in Italian history which turned a democracy into a fascist State. Within two years of becoming Italy's Prime Minister in 1922, Benito Mussolini abolished press freedom and all Opposition parties and established the Fascist Grand Council (*Gran Consiglio del Fascismo*) with the power to approve all constitutional amendments.

Having wrecked the foundations of Italian democracy, Mussolini equated himself with the State and declared, *"Tutto nello stato, Neinte al di fuori dello stato, Nulla contro lo stato."* (Everything within the State, Nothing outside the state, Nothing against the State). For long, members of the Congress Party have equated 'the family' with the State. Thus, for them, it has always been "Tutto nello famiglia, neinte aldi fuori dello famiglia, nulla contro lo famiglia" (Everything within the family, nothing outside the family, nothing against the family)!

Will Indians who live and breathe democracy accept this kind of *'parivarvaad'* in this time and age ? I doubt it.

Notes:

1. *My Presidential Years*, R. Venkataraman, HarperCollins, New Delhi-1994, pp. 89-90
2. H.R. Khanna, *Neither Roses Nor Thorns*, Eastern Book Company, Lucknow, pp. 78-79

❑❑❑